SACRAMENT SERIES

CONFIRMATION

Cardinal Jorge Medina Estévez
Foreword by Cardinal Angelo Sodano

Libreria Editrice Vaticana

United States Conference of Catholic Bishops
Washington, DC

First printing, February 2015

ISBN 978-1-60137-430-1

TABLE OF CONTENTS

FOREWORD

Cardinal Jorge Medina Estévez has given us his new booklet on a very important issue for the Christian life—the Sacrament of Confirmation. We are all very grateful for this. The new publication we have before us reveals once again the deep theological knowledge and the great apostolic spirit of this venerable pastor of the Church.

For my part, I would like to express my vote for the wide dissemination of this book, especially among young people, who can find in the Sacrament of Confirmation a special grace for becoming witnesses of Christ in today's world.

In addition, I would like to say that I wrote this foreword while an assembly of the Synod of Bishops was held in the Vatican, focusing on examining the theme of the New Evangelization for the transmission of the faith in today's world.

Well, during this assembly, many bishops coming from different continents mentioned the importance of the testimony that Christians should offer in order to bring men and women to acceptance of the gift of faith. It was then pointed out how the Sacrament of Confirmation has the precise role of giving a new gift to the person who was baptized, i.e., the strength to be able to bear witness to the world about their own faith. In fact, the Baptism makes us disciples of Christ, and Confirmation calls us to become Apostles. Through this Sacrament, the gifts of the Holy Spirit fall on us and "equip" us to carry out our apostolic mission in the world.

This way, we are from our youth to be the "salt of the earth" and "the light of the world" (Mt 5:13, 14) and to bring the "fire" of the Gospel of Christ to the earth (Lk 12:49).

Without doubt, the young people of today are confronted with many difficulties in order to be faithful to their mission. They can find comfort in Jesus' words to the Twelve during the Last Supper before his Passion: "In the world you will have trouble, but take courage, I have conquered the world" (Jn 16:33).

Cardinal Angelo Sodano
Dean of the College of Cardinals

From the Vatican, October 18, 2012,
Feast of St. Luke the Evangelist

WILL I RECEIVE THE SACRAMENT OF CONFIRMATION?

Introduction

Surely, you have heard that certain young adults will shortly "confirm their faith" and perhaps you have said yourself "I confirmed my faith in that place, on that day." In fact, this expression is not truly correct, because it is not you who confirms but God. Confirmation, as each sacrament through which God grants us his grace for our sanctification and ultimately for our eternal salvation, is a gift from God that must be received by men and women with the necessary disposition, and that does not come from us but from his loving mercy. The truth, therefore, is that God confirms "you" and it is not you who "confirms." You should therefore say, "I have been confirmed," or "I have received Confirmation." Of course, in this sacrament, as in all sacraments, the man or woman's disposition is important, but we must not forget that the initiative of salvation comes from God and it can come only from him.

An extensive and rich explanation about the doctrine of the Sacrament of Confirmation may be found in the *Catechism of the Catholic Church* between numbers 1285 and 1321. It is indispensable reading for anyone who wants to understand the authentic doctrine of the Church concerning Confirmation. This booklet does not pretend to do more than present this doctrine in a very simple form, suitable for every person.

Analyzing the Words

"Confirm" is very similar to "firm" and perhaps the prefix "with (*con* in Italian)" may suggest that the firmness is conferred *to* and *for a group* and not just to an individual. The "group" does not refer to those participating in the celebration but the ecclesial body, the whole Church.

"Reinforce," "strengthen," "consolidate," and "confirm" are words with similar meaning, indicating that something or someone has a certain firmness but not enough and not all that is needed in order to not need more. The idea of firmness has to do with the ability to withstand a certain amount of force, which acts in the opposite direction and which may destabilize that which opposes resistance.

Does the Christian find resistance in his or her life? Of course! Life on this earth is not easy. Moving forward requires effort and perseverance. Our nature, prone to laziness and to making the minimum of effort, has to be conquered and stimulated. The work is painful and unpleasant, and, often, adverse circumstances arise requiring no small effort to overcome. It would be extremely naïve to think that we can go forward without encountering stumbling blocks. The Book of Job is right in saying that human life is similar to that of a soldier (Cf. Jb 7:1); who does not know that the soldiers' lives imply continuous effort?

Our Enemies

According to the Christian faith, we know that we have powerful opponents: the Devil, whom Jesus calls "the enemy" (Cf. Mt 13:25), and his followers, which are continuously trying to make us stray from the path of salvation (Cf. Mk 4:15; Lk 22:31). Therefore, the life of the Christian cannot avoid the fight and the battle against Satan (Cf. Eph 6:10-20; 1 Pt 5:8).

The strategy used by the Devil to achieve his purpose and make us deviate from the path of salvation is the permanent appeal to lies, falsehood, and deceit. Jesus calls him "the father of lies" (Jn 8:44) and Sacred Scriptures clearly indicate that he is a liar. In paradise, when he tempted our ancestors, he did so by deceiving them; he made them believe that God was jealous and assured them that disobedience would have no negative consequence (Cf. Gen 3:1-4). When he tempted Jesus, the Devil assured Jesus falsely and with unthinkable boldness that the whole world belonged to him (Cf. Lk 4:5-7). All temptations have a foundation of falsehood, the rejection of the truth, and the presentation of misleading appearances as if they were the truth.

Jesus is the Truth, and for this reason, his work of salvation is accomplished through the proclamation of the Gospel. In his dialog with Pontius Pilate, the Lord told Pilate: "For this I was born and for this I came into the world, to testify to the truth. Everyone who belongs to the truth listens to my voice" (Jn 18:37). In the farewell speech at the end of the Last Supper, Jesus promised his disciples, "the Advocate, the holy Spirit that the Father will send in my name—he will teach you everything and remind you of all that [I] told you" (Jn 14:26). Shortly after that, he told them, "When the Advocate comes whom I will send you from the Father, the Spirit of truth that proceeds from the Father, he will testify to me. And you also testify, because you have been with me from the beginning" (Jn 15:26 f.).

It is important to emphasize that Jesus is the Truth and that one of the names of the Holy Spirit is specifically the *Spirit of Truth*, because it is clear that the Christian must be an irreconcilable enemy of falsehood and of Satan, the great liar. If lies and deception were not to reign in the world, as they unfortunately do, coexistance based on trust and fraternity among men and women would take the place of mistrust and suspicion, which in our days flood and poison the relations between individuals and between nations.

Therefore, no one should be surprised that the popes, both Saint John Paul II and his successor Pope Benedict XVI have stated that Christians must face the harsh reality of "going against the current," because the influence of the Devil is so great that St. John said in his First Letter: "The whole world is under the power of the evil one" (1 Jn 5:19). These words, inspired by the Holy Spirit, are not the expression of an insane pessimism but positive realism, because we are freed from the dangerous illusion that everything is going well and there are no grounds for serious concern. During the French Revolution, while the violence and killings were already getting out of control, a lady of company was trying to reassure her mistress by telling her: "There is nothing new!" It is said that the ostrich hides his head in the sand when danger approaches to avoid seeing the threat.

You Will Be My Witnesses

Jesus told his disciples before ascending to heaven: "But you will receive power when the holy Spirit comes upon you, and you will be my witnesses in Jerusalem, throughout Judea and Samaria, and to the ends of the earth" (Acts 1:8). These words set out a program, were prophetic, and established an apostolic and missionary mandate.

What is a witness? Someone who is sure and has no doubts about something, someone who is convinced of the truth of what he or she knows, someone who is willing to take risks and even suffer consequences for testifying, even publicly, about the truth of his or her words.

In Greek, the word *martyr* corresponds to the Italian word for *witness*. In all the centuries of Christianity there have been men and women, elderly and young, bishops, priests, deacons, and lay people, who, when they had to choose between losing life in the body for openly and courageously confessing their faith or preserving their earthly life by paying the price of renouncing their Christian faith, preferred to bear witness to their faith, even if they had to pay for it by shedding their blood. These are the real *witnesses* and *martyrs* and their blood was and will always be the seed that makes fruitful the new Christians. The Christian who bears constantly the Cross of Christ (Cf. Mt 10:38; Mk 8:34) in all his or her activities in the family, at work, and in his or her professional and social life gives a valuable witness of what it means "to live by faith," as defined by St. Paul (Cf. Rm 1:17; Gal 3:11; Heb 10:38).

On the contrary, the Christian who shows inconsistency between his or her behavior and faith gives a *counter-testimony* that can influence other men and women to despise the Christian faith or even to "blaspheme the name of God," according to the harsh judgment of the Apostle (Cf. Rm 2:24; 14:16; 1 Tim 6:1).

Our life is therefore the first form of apostolic mandate. Pope Paul VI used to say that our world has an urgent need for witnesses, and not only for teachers, because sometimes the fine words and arguments of someone who "teaches" remain without effect because of his or her conduct. In fact, Jesus, rebuking some of his contemporaries, said, "Therefore, do and observe all things whatsoever they tell you, but do not follow their example. For they preach but they do not practice" (Mt 23:3).

We Christians cannot circumvent the pressing questions that follow: Am I really a credible witness, or on the contrary, do I discredit with my actions the Christian faith that I professed with my mouth? Do I show a "split personality," following some of the Catholic teachings on morality but ignoring others? According to its Greek root, the word "scandal" means "stumbling block." To "scandalize" means to "put stumbling blocks" in the life of other Christians, causing them to do what is wrong because of the bad examples that we give them. Do I cause somebody to sin with my inconsistent conduct?

Witnesses to What?

— That God exists, that nothing is unknown to him, and that he is of utmost importance in the life of every human being;

— That everything is necessarily related to him and without him everything becomes a blur and loses its meaning;

— That the eternal Son of God became man in Mary's pure womb and that his name is Jesus;
— That Jesus is our only Savior and that there is no salvation outside him, because he shed his blood for all;
— That the Gospel of Jesus is the supreme truth and whatever contradicts the Gospel is a lie and destroys men and women;
— That Jesus is risen, alive, and glorious in heaven, together with the Father and the Holy Spirit, but is also present among us;
— That Jesus lives and acts in his Church, through his Word, his sacraments, the pastoral service of his ministers, and the holiness of all those who belong to the ecclesial body;
— That the commandments included in the Law of God are all, without exception, an authentic expression of humanity and the only way to realize the true brotherhood of mankind;
— That every Christian is a servant and that serving is more important than to be served;
— That there is more joy in giving than in receiving and that God loves those who are joyful givers;
— That we must treat others as we want to be treated by others and that we must never do to others what we do not want others to do to us;
— That to love is to give oneself, freely, generously, and cheerfully;

- — That rights and obligations are related, so when we talk about rights, we talk also of obligations and that without accepting the obligations, rights lead to unhealthy selfishness;
- — That the truth makes us free, while the lie enslaves us;
- — That every human being bears the image of Christ and deserves love and respect, despite his or her shortcomings;
- — That we are sinners in need of God's grace and forgiveness and that we must be willing to forgive those who have offended us or caused us harm, in order to be forgiven;
- — That daily work is not a curse but a gift from God to earn our livelihood, to serve our neighbor, to help the poor, and to be able to accomplish our full potential;
- — That our life on earth is important but is not our final destination, therefore we will make a joyful effort in its pursuit, while remaining aware that it is only a first step, a provisional one, before reaching the fullness of life, which is eternal.

Does this list of testimonies seem long to you? We could add many more, but in reality, this list is nothing but the breakdown of the fundamental testimony, about loving God above all things, and loving our neighbor as we love ourselves (Cf. Mt 22:37-40). This list is not more than a reminder, or if you prefer, an examination of conscience, which you can follow.

You might say that it is not easy to give this testimony, and I agree with you. Indeed, we must recognize that, with human effort alone (Cf. Jn 15:4 f.), and due to the bad influences around us, it may be impossible. But if we follow the teachings of St. Paul and believe that "all things are possible" through Christ who sustains us (Cf. Phil 4:13), we have the absolute and comforting certainty that it is possible to give Christian witness *with* and *through* the grace of God. If this were not so, Jesus would not have made this an indispensable obligation in order to be his disciples.

The Weakness of the Apostles

The Apostles and the disciples of Jesus were weak, and there are quite a few examples of this in the Gospels. They thought that his kingdom would be similar to the kingdoms of this world, having a political character (Cf. Lk 24:17-24), and they hoped to be given positions that were humanly advantageous (Cf. Mt 20:20-28). They were discussing among themselves who would have the highest positions in it (Cf. Mk 9:33-37; 10:35-45; Lk 22:24 ff.). Peter, and probably all the others, could not understand the mystery of salvation through the Cross (Cf. Mt 16:22), and because of this, he was harshly rebuked by the Lord (Cf. Mt 16:23). At the time of Jesus' arrest, everyone fled and abandoned him (Cf. Mt 26:56), and Peter denied him (Cf. Mt 26:69-75; Mk 14:66-72; Lk 22:55-62; Jn 18:15-25). In fact, it was one of them, Judas Iscariot, who cowardly betrayed him, being bribed with thirty miserable silver coins (Cf. Mt 26:14-16; Mk 14:10 f.; Lk 22:3-6). Only one of the Twelve Apostles, John, was present at the Cross (Cf. Jn 19:26 f.). Even after the Resurrection of the Lord, some continued to doubt him (Cf. Mt 28:17).

The weaknesses and lack of courage of the Apostles and disciples clearly contrast with the faithfulness of other individuals. First of all with that of the Blessed Virgin Mary, the Apostle John, the other holy women who accompanied Jesus to the Cross (Cf. Jn 19:25), and with that of two eminent Jews, Nicodemus and Joseph of Arimathea, who carried his inert body and gave him a honorable burial (Cf. Jn 19:38-42).

After the Resurrection, the Apostles were still afraid of the Jews (Cf. Jn 20:19).

The weaknesses and the lack of courage of the Apostles teach us many lessons. In the first place, we learn that Jesus wished to establish his Church using people who had shortcomings and weaknesses and who lacked courage. Why? First of all, to admonish us concerning pride and to teach us that *without Him we can do nothing* (Cf. Jn 15:5) and that *we cannot take credit for anything as coming from us; rather, our qualification comes from God* (Cf. 2 Cor 3:7). Therefore, any vainglory is cut off at the root and we make our journey aware of our total wretchedness and trusting only in the power of God. In addition, it shows us that despite our weakness, the Lord does not reject us but mercifully offers us his forgiveness and desires to continue to rely on us. This was very clear in Peter's case, who despite cowardly denying Jesus (Cf. Jn 18:15 ff.) was confirmed by Jesus in his high and special pastoral mission after Peter declared his love three times, humbled himself (Cf. Jn 21:15-19), and was not presumptuous by comparing himself to others (Cf. Mt 26:33-35).

Pentecost

Everything changes on the day of Pentecost:

> When the time for Pentecost was fulfilled, they were all in one place together. And suddenly there came from the sky a

noise like a strong driving wind, and it filled the entire house in which they were. Then there appeared to them tongues as of fire, which parted and came to rest on each one of them. And they were all filled with the holy Spirit and began to speak in different tongues as the Spirit enabled them to proclaim. Now there were devout Jews from every nation under heaven staying in Jerusalem.

At this sound, they gathered in a large crowd, but they were confused because each one heard them speaking in his own language. They were astounded, and in amazement they asked, "Are not all these who are speaking Galileans? Then how does each of us hear them in his own native language?" . . . Then Peter stood up with the Eleven, raised his voice, and proclaimed to them, "You who are Jews, indeed all of you staying in Jerusalem. Let this be known to you, and listen to my words. These people are not drunk, as you suppose, for it is only nine o'clock in the morning. No, this is what was spoken through the prophet Joel: 'It will come to pass in the last days,' God says, 'that I will pour out a portion of my spirit upon all flesh. Your sons and your daughters shall prophesy, your young men shall see visions, your old men shall dream dreams. Indeed, upon my servants and my handmaids I will pour out a portion of my spirit in those days, and they shall prophesy.'" (Acts 2:1-8, 14-18)

From that moment, the Apostles' fear disappears, and they begin wholeheartedly the evangelization of all peoples and nations. They will do so with determination, with perseverance, and with a holy boldness. They will find harsh resistance and will suffer violent persecutions, and even death, at the hand of those who hate the Gospel.

The Church, following the writings of the prophet Isaiah (Cf. Is 11:1 f.), attributes to the Holy Spirit the granting of seven "gifts": *wisdom, understanding, counsel, fortitude, knowledge, piety, and the fear of the Lord* (Cf. *Catechism of the Catholic Church*, no. 1831). Some of these gifts refer to docility, accepting the truth and discerning it from error; others refer to the will, accepting lovingly the will of God.

Generally, we consider *wisdom* to be the way we perceive the realities that surround us, not according to the false standards of the world, which include falsehood, selfishness, materialism, pride, and violence but from the perspective of the Gospel, using truth, humility, a spirit of service, and meekness. From a Christian standpoint, a person is not wise who possesses a large amount of knowledge but who learns to see things the way God sees and considers them.

Fortitude is steadfastness when faced with difficulties, perseverance to wait for things that cannot be obtained immediately, and the integrity and determination to face suffering, especially when it comes as a consequence for choosing an attitude consistent with the Gospel.

Every Christian needs to be *wise* and *strong*; these virtues and gifts are the fruit and grace of the Holy Spirit's action.

After Pentecost

There are two passages in the Sacred Scripture that show how the Apostles understood from the beginnings of the Church's life that one of their pastoral responsibilities was to impart to the faithful the gift of the Holy Spirit.

Here's the first: "Now when the apostles in Jerusalem heard that Samaria had accepted the word of God, they sent them Peter and John, who went down and prayed for them, that they might receive the holy Spirit; for it had not yet fallen upon any of them; they had only been baptized in the name of the Lord Jesus. Then they laid hands on them and they received the holy Spirit" (Acts 8.14-17).

The second:

Paul traveled through the interior of the country and came (down) to Ephesus where he found some disciples. He said to them, "Did you receive the holy Spirit when you became believers?" They answered him, "We have never even heard that there is a holy Spirit." He said, "How were you baptized?" They replied, "With the baptism of John." Paul then said, "John baptized with a baptism of repentance, telling the people to believe in the one who was to come after him, that is, in Jesus." When they heard this, they were baptized in the name of the Lord Jesus. And when Paul laid [his] hands on them, the holy Spirit came upon them, and they spoke in tongues and prophesied. Altogether there were about twelve men. (Acts 19:1-7)

Christian initiation had two starting points, *Baptism* and the *impartation of the Holy Spirit*, the latter reserved to the Apostles. This impartation of the Holy Spirit was called the *Sacrament of Confirmation* in the ancient liturgical tradition of the Church.

Who Has the Mandate of Conferring the Sacrament of Confirmation?

In the Eastern Churches, in which by liturgical tradition the Sacraments of Baptism, Confirmation, and first Eucharist are celebrated together, also for children, these three Sacraments of Christian Initiation are administered by the one presiding over the celebration, either a bishop or a presbyter (priest).

In the Latin Church, the ordinary minister of Confirmation is the diocesan bishop. If for grave reasons he cannot administer it personally, he should ask another bishop who is available to celebrate it. If there are no bishops available, the diocesan bishop may authorize one or more priests to administer the Sacrament of Confirmation, to ensure that the faithful are not being deprived of the grace of this sacrament.

When a Christian, adult or child, is in danger of death, the Church authorizes any priest to administer the Sacrament of Confirmation without asking for any authorization. This pastoral authorization is based on the desire of the Church that none of her children depart this world without having received the grace of Confirmation, which will confer on him or her greater glory in eternal bliss.

The celebrating minister must wear the liturgically appropriate sacred vestments, which symbolize that he acts, not by virtue of his quality or personal identity, but in the name and the authority of Jesus Christ, who is the true author of grace, and that the minister is only his tool.

Where and When Is the Sacrament of Confirmation Celebrated?

Normally, the celebration of the Sacrament of Confirmation must take place in a church, unless a large number of the faithful are present or there is a serious reason that makes it advisable to choose another place; this place has to be appropriate and the necessary precautions have to be taken to avoid noises that may disturb the celebration or that may be incompatible with the respect due to its sacred character.

The celebration must be well prepared, if possible with a rehearsal attended by the candidates for Confirmation and their sponsors. The church must be prepared as for a day of great celebration. Those who will receive Confirmation must be dressed soberly and decently, avoiding excessively expensive or flashy clothing. The music must be adequate, mentioning the Holy Spirit and the responsibility of every Christian to be a witness.

As provided in the liturgy, the celebration of the Sacrament of Confirmation should normally take place during the Holy Mass. The Scripture passages relevant to the Eucharistic Celebration highlight the action of the Holy Spirit and prepare participants to receive the sacrament more fruitfully. In addition, the celebration of Holy Mass expresses the unity of the three Sacraments of Christian Initiation: Baptism, Confirmation, and Eucharist. In fact, during this time those who are confirmed renew the promises of Baptism and draw near to receive the Body and the Blood of the Lord through the Holy Eucharist.

In general, the celebration of Confirmation on Sundays is not recommended because of its duration, which is longer than that of the ordinary celebration of the Holy Mass, and may cause problems in the administration of Sunday Eucharist, causing delays and inconvenience to the faithful who are participating.

What Is the Essential Rite of Confirmation?

In formulating this question, we do not try to suggest in any way that one can neglect the rites as a whole, as they are all important and are part of the celebration, or that we can omit or change some of them capriciously. It is required to invite all those present, especially those who receive the sacrament, to pay particular attention and have a favorable disposition for receiving the grace of Confirmation.

The central moment of the celebration is when the celebrant, having dipped the thumb of his right hand in the sacred chrism, anoints the forehead of the candidate with a sign in the shape of a cross, pronouncing at the same time the words: "Be sealed with the gift of the Holy Spirit." The candidate to Confirmation responds "Amen," and the celebrant gives him or her a sign or kiss of peace, saying, "Peace be with you," and the candidate to Confirmation responds, "And with your spirit." The sign of peace expresses the ecclesial communion of the person being confirmed with the bishop and with all the faithful members of the Church. Then the newly confirmed and his or her godfather or godmother (sponsors) return to their seats.

The sacred chrism is oil, if possible olive oil, blended with fragrant balm, blessed by the diocesan bishop in his cathedral during the so-named "Chrism Mass," which is celebrated every year on Holy Thursday. The sacred chrism is used in the celebration of the Baptism of infants, by anointing their heads immediately after the water of Baptism is poured on their heads. As explained before, it is also used in the celebration of the Sacrament of Confirmation, and in the ordination of the bishops, who receive an anointing on their foreheads, and in the ordination of the priests, who receive an anointing on the palms of their hands.

All of these anointings that occur in the liturgy of the Church are symbolic. They suggest joy, a gift of the grace of God, protection against the snares of the Devil, consecration to the glory of God, and purification of the traces left by personal sins. In the case of the sacred chrism, its perfume symbolizes the vocation of every Christian to spread around him or her, by words and attitudes, "the fragrance of Christ," as explained by St. Paul: "For we are the aroma of Christ for God" (2 Cor 2:15), an idea that suggests the offerings in the Old Covenant, the expression of a life pleasing to the eyes of God (Cf. Es 30:1-37; Rm 12:1).

The Christian who is inconsistent in his or her faith because of living a life visibly in contradiction with the Law of God and who is far from spreading the aroma of Christ through his or her life diffuses the stench of Satan, causing great harm to the human community and to the Church.

Who Can and Should Receive Confirmation?

Since Baptism is the basis of the whole Christian life and implies the desire for all the graces that God grants us to live in a way that is consistent with the Gospel, receiving the Sacrament of Confirmation is the natural consequence of having received Baptism. Therefore, Confirmation is not an "optional" sacrament and receiving it does not depend on the desire of the baptized Christian. If one refuses to receive Confirmation, they objectively and regrettably reject God's grace.

Now is the time to develop an idea expressed in the first pages of this booklet.

Every sacrament is a gift of God, a free gift that he gives us through his Church, so that we grow as disciples of Christ, for our personal sanctification and for fulfilling the responsibility of every Christian toward the salvation of our brothers and sisters. For this reason, the refusal of Confirmation is similar to "truncating" the baptismal vocation and refusing the fullness to which God calls us, accepting and desiring instead the condition of "stunted" members of his Church. Certainly, this is a clear inconsistency and a sign of lack of wisdom!

Sometimes we hear people who are new in the faith saying that Confirmation is the moment in which a young man or a young woman decides if they want to be Christian or not. If such an idea were acceptable, which according to the Catholic doctrine it is certainly not, it would mean that Baptism is only "provisional" and needs further ratification to be valid, just as it would mean that first Communion and all other Eucharistic Communions received before Confirmation are only "provisional." Therefore, what is the purpose of being baptized and having received so many times the Sacred Body of Jesus? Is it possible to cancel all of these as something without value and meaning a few years later when the time comes for Confirmation, if Confirmation is not received?

This type of reasoning is based on a false interpretation of the idea of freedom, which certainly does not consist in freedom of doing what we want, perhaps even something objectively bad, but in the adherence to what is good, which is the only choice that can bring true freedom and happiness. Choosing what is evil is not strictly an act of freedom, but a deformed and defective use of our capacity to choose. It is as if limping were considered the correct and ideal way to exercise the ability to move.

Let us look at this more in depth. According to the teachings of St. Paul, the Father in heaven has chosen us in Christ, "before the foundation of the world, to be holy and without blemish before him. In love he destined us for adoption to himself through Jesus Christ, in accord with the favor of his will, for the praise of the glory of his grace that he granted us in the beloved" (Eph 1:4-6). It is therefore a free choice of God, something that we did not deserve or desire but that is a gift of God's love for our good. Rejecting it would be an ingratitude and a fall into the deception of Satan, which means that we would seek our well-being where it is not and cannot be found.

What should we think of those who believe Confirmation is optional and not a continuation of the true life that we have freely received through Baptism? First of all, we should lament their error and with patience and sensitivity ensure that they understand the true meaning of the Christian life based on the free initiative of God. Furthermore, we must show them that the path of the Christian life does not consist in a reduction or in an attack on freedom but in achieving its highest expression. However, we do have to respect them, since it is possible that their error is either unintentional or without guilt. In addition, the Church does not allow forcing the person to receive Confirmation against his or her will if they do not desire to receive it.

Concerning the appropriate age for receiving Confirmation,

there have been and still are several criteria and liturgical practices. In the Eastern Churches, which confer together in the same celebration the three sacraments of Christian initiation—Baptism, Confirmation, and Eucharist—the problem is already solved. The same happens in the Latin Church when it comes to the Baptism of an adult, since the liturgical norms in this case prescribe the administration of Confirmation and the Eucharist in the same celebration.

In recent times, in different dioceses, the natural order of the Sacraments of Christian Initiation was reestablished, placing Confirmation before first Communion. In such circumstances, the age at which someone may receive Confirmation oscillates between the age of eight and ten years and after which children receive their first Eucharist, as established by St. Pius X. In some countries, Confirmation is delayed until the children are at least fifteen years of age, because at this age a greater maturity is expected of the candidates. In this regard, it is appropriate to recall what the *Catechism of the Catholic Church* says: "Although Confirmation is sometimes called the 'sacrament of Christian maturity,' we must not confuse adult faith with the adult age of natural growth, nor forget that the baptismal grace is a grace of free, unmerited election and does not need 'ratification' to become effective" (no. 1308). The same paragraph of the *Catechism* cites St. Thomas Aquinas, who reminds us that "many children, through the strength of the Holy Spirit they have received, have bravely fought for Christ even to the shedding of their blood." The blessed adolescents Laura Vicuña and Ceferino Namuncurá received their Confirmation as children.

In order to receive Confirmation fruitfully, the candidate to Confirmation must be in a state of grace and therefore, if he or she has reached the age of reason, the candidate has to receive first the Sacrament of Penance or Reconciliation. Of course, this does not apply in case of the adult who receives Baptism, Confirmation, and the Eucharist together, because the Sacrament of Baptism cleanses all the sins that the candidate has previously committed.

Those who desire to receive Confirmation must prepare properly, following the provisions of the diocese in which they live. The preparation consists in catechesis on the Christian life and not only on the Sacrament of Confirmation. It must be appropriate to the age and the circumstances of the candidates. The preparation is important but does not itself guarantee a future as a Christian to those who receive this sacrament. St. Augustine was right to show that just as a good person on whom great hopes are pinned may become corrupt and disappoint with the passing of time, so may someone who is far from living a model of Christian life be redeemed and become an excellent disciple of Christ. This is the mystery of grace and human frailty.

The Sacrament of Confirmation imprints on the soul of the confirmed a seal, a sign or "character" that is indelible and therefore it can only be received once in a lifetime. The same happens with the Sacraments of Baptism and Holy Orders, through which a "character" is imprinted. The fact that these sacraments impart an indelible sign does not mean that their effectiveness is limited to the moment in which the sacraments are received; they continue to impart grace and salvation throughout life. We can compare them to the "solar batteries" with which some tools are provided:

when they are in darkness, "they rest," but when they receive light, they transform it into the energy that makes them function.

The Sponsors

The candidate to Confirmation should be accompanied by a sponsor; however, this provision is not an absolute necessity, because if the appropriate person for this responsibility is not found, one can do without.

The role of the sponsor is not a purely social commitment or friendship. The person who assumes this commitment must be a Christian who lives a life of faith and whose moral conduct is irreproachable. He or she must be an observant Catholic, who has received the Sacrament of Confirmation. The responsibility of the sponsor is to support the candidate in his or her Christian life, both by the sponsor's own example and with words and advice. Therefore, it is unacceptable for the sponsor to be a person of bad reputation or publicly known for his or her lack of honesty or who lives in fornication or adultery. If the person has such shortcomings or moral weaknesses, he or she cannot be a sponsor entrusted with this task.

If possible, it is appropriate that the baptismal godfather or godmother also be the Confirmation sponsor to emphasize the unity between these two sacraments.

In many places, the sponsor pronounces the name of the candidate immediately before the minister anoints the candidate with the sacred chrism. In other places, the candidate to Confirmation wears on his or her chest a card with his or her name, so that the celebrant may pronounce it at the time of the anointing. This is very practical, because it avoids confusion of names, especially for names that are not very common. When the celebrant anoints the forehead of the person who receives the sacrament, the sponsor, standing behind him, must place his or her right hand on the right shoulder of the candidate.

The Fruits, Graces, and Effects of Confirmation

The sacramental words pronounced by the bishop or the priest who celebrates the Sacrament of Confirmation, "Be sealed with the gift of the Holy Spirit," may be translated, as was done in other languages, as "Receive the gift of God, which is the Holy Spirit."

The fruits of Confirmation can be described by saying that the Holy Spirit is poured out in a special way on the one who receives this sacrament, as it was poured out at Pentecost, when it descended on the Apostles. It gives abundance, growth, strength, and deepens the baptismal grace, which it completes.

The *Catechism of the Catholic Church* describes the effects of Confirmation as follows:

— "It roots us more deeply in the divine filiation which makes us cry: 'Abba, Father' "(Rom 8:15);
— "Unites us more firmly to Christ";
— "It increases the gifts of the Holy Spirit in us";
— "It renders our bond with the Church more perfect";
— "It gives us a special strength of the Holy Spirit to spread and defend the faith by word and action as true witnesses of Christ, to confess the name of Christ boldly, and never to be ashamed of his Cross" (no. 1303);
— "This 'character' perfects the common priesthood of the faithful, received in Baptism, and 'the confirmed person

receives the power to profess faith in Christ publicly, and as it were officially'" (no. 1305), according to the teachings of St. Thomas Aquinas.

What a joy it is to know that there are many persons who are baptized and then receive the Sacrament of Confirmation, and how sad it is that there are others, who do not have the opportunity to receive it, and others, who do not do so out of ignorance or negligence! What a beautiful day of celebration it is for a parish, school, or small community when some of their faithful receive the sacrament of wisdom, of strength, and of becoming a witness!

Conclusion

This old bishop, to whom the Lord has granted the joy of administering the Sacrament of Confirmation to about 40,000 Catholics (this is not very much, because St. Toribio de Mogrovejo, zealous Archbishop of Lima, administered it to approximately 600,000 persons during his twenty-five years of episcopal ministry, making pastoral visits and traveling about 20,000 miles on foot or by mule), invites you, if you are not confirmed yet, to get prepared and receive the sacrament, and if you are already confirmed, to revitalize in yourself the precious fruits of this great sacrament.

Finally, please remember the heroic examples of the saints, who showed strength and perseverance in their love toward God and their neighbor. Remember the Old Testament, the seven Maccabee brothers who were martyrs and their heroic mother, who encouraged them to defend the faith and not fear death at the hands of their persecutor (Cf. 2 Mac 7:1-42); remember the elderly St. Eleazar, who, already ninety years old, sealed his long and exemplary life of faith in God with his own martyrdom (Cf. 2 Mac 6:18-31); remember the saints and martyrs, Apostles of Jesus Christ, and all the Christian martyrs, among them the holy deacon and martyr Stephen and the holy bishops and martyrs, Ignatius of Antioch and Polycarp of Smyrna; remember the martyr girl St. Agnes, whose tiny hands could not be held fast by the iron chains; remember the faithful slave St. Felicity, given up to death for having confessed her faith, only seven days after giving birth to her baby; remember the soldier-martyrs of the famous Tebea Legion, faithful to the emperor, but more faithful to Christ. Making a great leap in history, we remember the martyrs who shed their blood in the early years of the Church in China, Japan, Vietnam, and Korea. And if we make another leap, we remember the many dozens of martyrs killed during the violent persecution in Mexico at the beginning of the twentieth century. We cannot forget the heroic charity of the martyr St. Maximilian Kolbe or that of the priest St. Damien de Veuster, who in his love for Christ became a leper among the lepers and died terribly disfigured from that cruel disease. Let us remember the indigenous St. Juan Diego, whom God gave the grace to see the first apparition of the Virgin Mary in America, and who after seeing the apparition spent long years humbly caring for the small sanctuary dedicated to her. We also remember with admiration the heroic adolescent St. Maria Goretti, who defended her virginal chastity with courage, dying as a martyr stabbed over a dozen times and who, before her death, forgave generously her murderer and told him that she wanted to see him close to her in heaven. We cannot forget St. Gianna Beretta, doctor by profession, who refused to have an abortion and who, loving the son she was carrying in her womb, died shortly after birth. Let us remember the great educator St. John Bosco and let us not forget St. John Mary Vianney, the zealous Curé of Ars, who used to dedicate up to sixteen hours a day to listening to confessions. We also remember the wonderful example of the holy conjugal love of the parents of St. Thérèse of the Child Jesus, the Blessed Louis Martin and his wife, Blessed Marie Zelie Guerin, as well as the Italian couple, the Blessed Luigi Beltrame Quattrocchi and his wife Blessed Maria Corsini. All these saints, and so many others, were brave witnesses to the faith and to the Gospel and await us in the Father's house in heaven.

Please forgive me for taking so much time with this mini-list, certainly incomplete, of saints of every type. You may argue that other names are perhaps more emblematic, and I agree, but I mention these saints to encourage you, all Christians, and myself on the path, which is not always easy, to follow Jesus, the eternal Son of the Father, our Master and Savior.

I finish with a dear and filial affection toward the Blessed Virgin Mary, who conceived the Son of God as man in her most pure womb, through the work of the Holy Spirit (Cf. Lk 1:35) and was with the Apostles (Cf. Acts 2:1-47) when they were praying and awaiting the coming of the Holy Spirit. We beseech her with confidence to obtain the grace to be faithful and obedient to the life-giving Spirit and not to grieve him (Cf. Eph 4:30) with our hardness of heart (Cf. Ez 11:19 ff.)